Team Stats—Basketball Edition

PHILADELPHIA 76ers

Nicki Clausen-Grace
and Jeff Grace

BLACK
RABBIT
BOOKS

Bolt is published by Black Rabbit Books
P.O. Box 3263, Mankato, Minnesota, 56002.
www.blackrabbitbooks.com

Jennifer Besel, editor; Michael Sellner, designer;
Omay Ayres, photo researcher

Library of Congress Cataloging-in-Publication Data
Names: Clausen-Grace, Nicki, author. | Grace, Jeff, 1967- author.
Title: Philadelphia 76ers / by Nicki Clausen-Grace and Jeff Grace.
Description: Mankato, Minnesota : Black Rabbit Books, 2021. |
Series: Bolt. Team stats, Basketball edition | Includes bibliographical references and index. |
Audience: Ages 8-12 | Audience: Grades 4-6 |
Summary: "Discover the Philadelphia 76ers' powerhouse players and biggest moments through exciting text and dynamic infographics"— Provided by publisher.
Identifiers: LCCN 2019051130 (print) | LCCN 2019051131 (ebook) |
ISBN 9781623102951 (hardback) | ISBN 9781644663912 (paperback) |
ISBN 9781623103897 (ebook)
Subjects: LCSH: Philadelphia 76ers (Basketball team)—History—Juvenile literature.
Classification: LCC GV885.52.P45 C53 2021 (print) | LCC GV885.52.P45 (ebook) | DDC 796.323/640974811—dc23
LC record available at https://lccn.loc.gov/2019051130
LC ebook record available at https://lccn.loc.gov/2019051131

Printed in the United States. 2/20

All facts and statistics are current as of the 2018–2019 season.

Image Credits

achievement.org: Academy of Acheivement, 4; AP Images: Al Messerschmidt Archive, 22–23; ASSOCIATED PRESS, 10, 12, 13; Charles Bennett, 19; Chris Szagola, 8, 26; GEORGE WIDMAN, 25; Kyusung Gong, 15; Matt Slocum, Cover; Michael Perez, 16; RUSTY KENNEDY, 14; Tom DiPace, 15; bleacherreport.com: Bleacher Report, 10–11; commons.wikimedia.org: Keith Allison, 15; Getty: Bettmann, 7, 19, 20–21, 22; Dmytro Aksonov, 14–15; Newscom: John E. Sokolowski, 28–29; picsart.com: Kicks'n Treys, 3; Shutterstock: Duda Vasilii, 28–29; EFKS, Cover, 1; GOLFX, 31; IfH, Cover; vasosh, 6, 9, 21, 28–29, 32; steinersports.com: Steiner Sports Memorabilia, 18; twitter.com: Philadelphia 76ers, 7

CONTENTS

FORUM
FORUM
LAKERS
31
SIXERS
6
SIXERS
45

CHAPTER 1

On the COURT

In 1983, the Philadelphia 76ers played the Los Angeles Lakers. 76ers player Julius Erving grabbed the ball. He dribbled down the court. He cradled the ball with his arm. Then he rocked the ball and threw down a slam dunk. Fans loved the showy score. And the move got its own nickname. It became "Rock the Baby."

CHAPTER 2

History of the 76ers

The 76ers formed in 1939. The team was called the Syracuse Nationals. In 1963, it moved to Philadelphia. In Philadelphia, the team became the 76ers. Since then, the team has won two NBA championships.

1967 World Champions

Joel Embiid
Ben Simmons

On the Money

In 2018, the 76ers team was worth $1.65 billion. That was the 12th highest in the NBA. The team's **net worth** doubled in just three years. New superstars Joel Embiid and Ben Simmons draw fans to the games. Fans pay to watch games. They also buy things with team **logos**.

In the 2017–2018 season, fans bought a lot of Embiid and Simmons jerseys. Both ranked in the top 10 for NBA jersey sales.

CHAPTER 3

Greatest MOMENTS

76ers history is made up of memorable moments. One of those moments was the 1967 NBA Finals. The 76ers played the San Francisco Warriors. The 76ers led three games to two. In Game 6, it was behind starting the fourth quarter. The players fought hard. With 15 seconds left, a 76er missed a shot. Wilt Chamberlain grabbed the **rebound** and put it in. The 76ers took the lead. The team won the NBA title.

PHILA
13

In the 1983 All-Star Game, three of the five starters were 76ers.

Stepped Up

It was Game 4 of the 1983 NBA Finals. The 76ers needed one more win. The players stepped up. Julius Erving scored 21 points. He also had five rebounds and six **assists**. Moses Malone added 24 points and 23 rebounds. They led the 76ers to a 115–108 victory.

Not Stopping Short

Allen Iverson is only 6 feet (1.8 meters) tall. That's on the short side for pro players. But he never let his height stop him. On February 12, 2005, Iverson was on fire. He sank 17 shots. And made many free throws. In total, he scored 60 points that game.

ALLEN IVERSON
6 feet, 0 inches (1.8 m)

Comparing Heights of NBA Stars

STEPHEN CURRY	MICHAEL JORDAN	LEBRON JAMES	SHAQUILLE O'NEAL
6 feet, 3 inches (1.9 m)	6 feet, 6 inches (1.9 m)	6 feet, 8 inches (2.0 m)	7 feet, 1 inch (2.2 m)

Sixers
25

A Sweet Game

On February 14, 2018, things didn't look good for the 76ers. It was playing the Miami Heat. It trailed by 23 points at halftime. Ben Simmons led a furious second half comeback. That game, he scored 18 points and grabbed 12 rebounds. He dished out 10 assists. His triple-double helped the team win.

triple-double — scoring at least 10 points, 10 rebounds, and 10 assists in a game

CHAPTER 4

76ers Superstars

It takes amazing players to make great plays. The team has had a lot of superstars over the years. Julius Erving was famous for his windmill dunks. He was also a great jumper. These skills led him to be on the NBA All-Star Team 11 times. He also helped the 76ers win an NBA championship in 1983.

76ers' Career Leaders

Hal Greer
most points
21,586

Julius Erving
most blocked shots
1,263

Maurice Cheeks
most assists
6,212

76ers Team Records

By the Numbers

68

most **wins** in a season

162–100

score of biggest **win**

93–149

score of biggest **loss**

163 most points scored in a game

9 fewest wins in a season

57 fewest points scored in a game

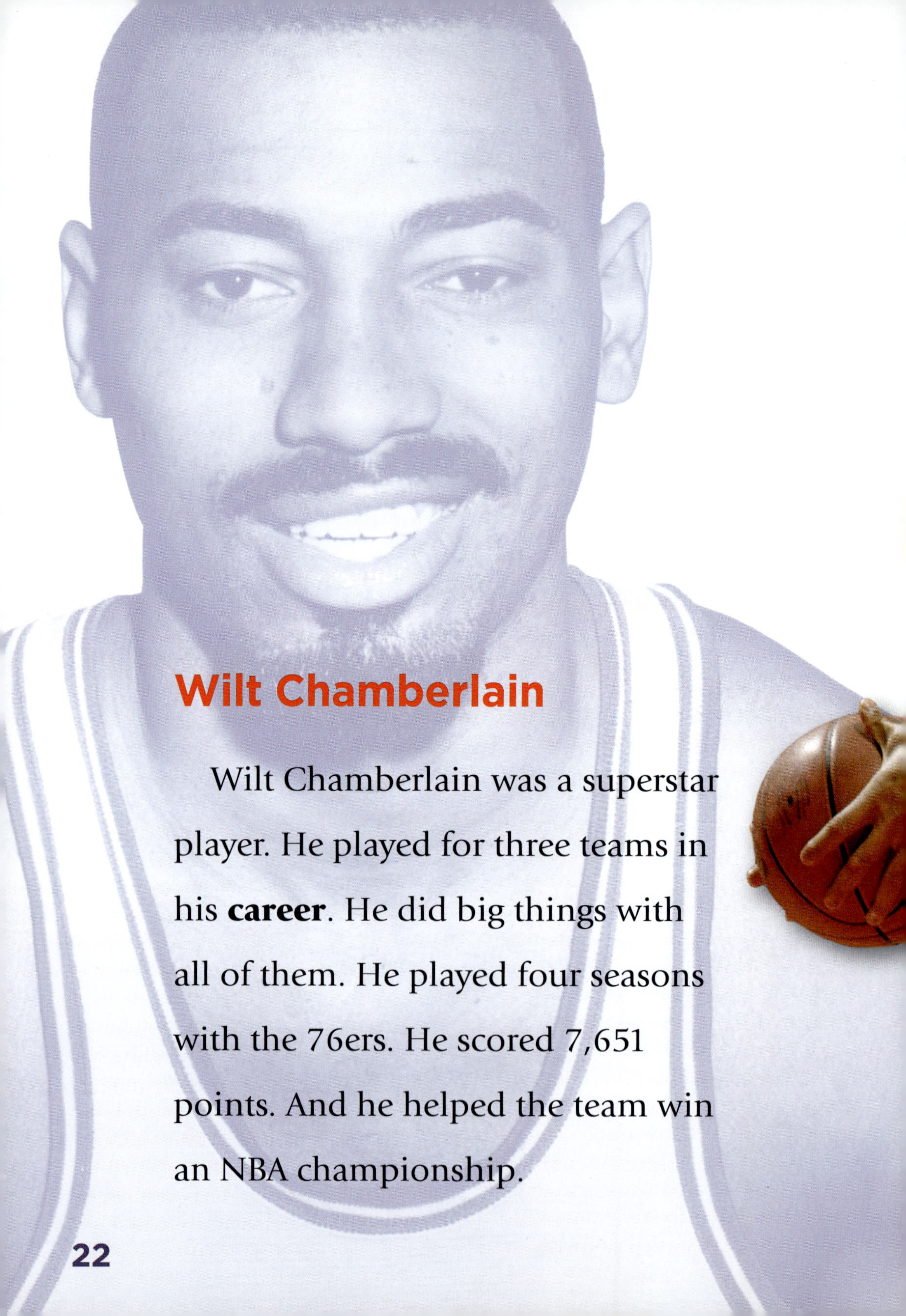

Wilt Chamberlain

Wilt Chamberlain was a superstar player. He played for three teams in his **career**. He did big things with all of them. He played four seasons with the 76ers. He scored 7,651 points. And he helped the team win an NBA championship.

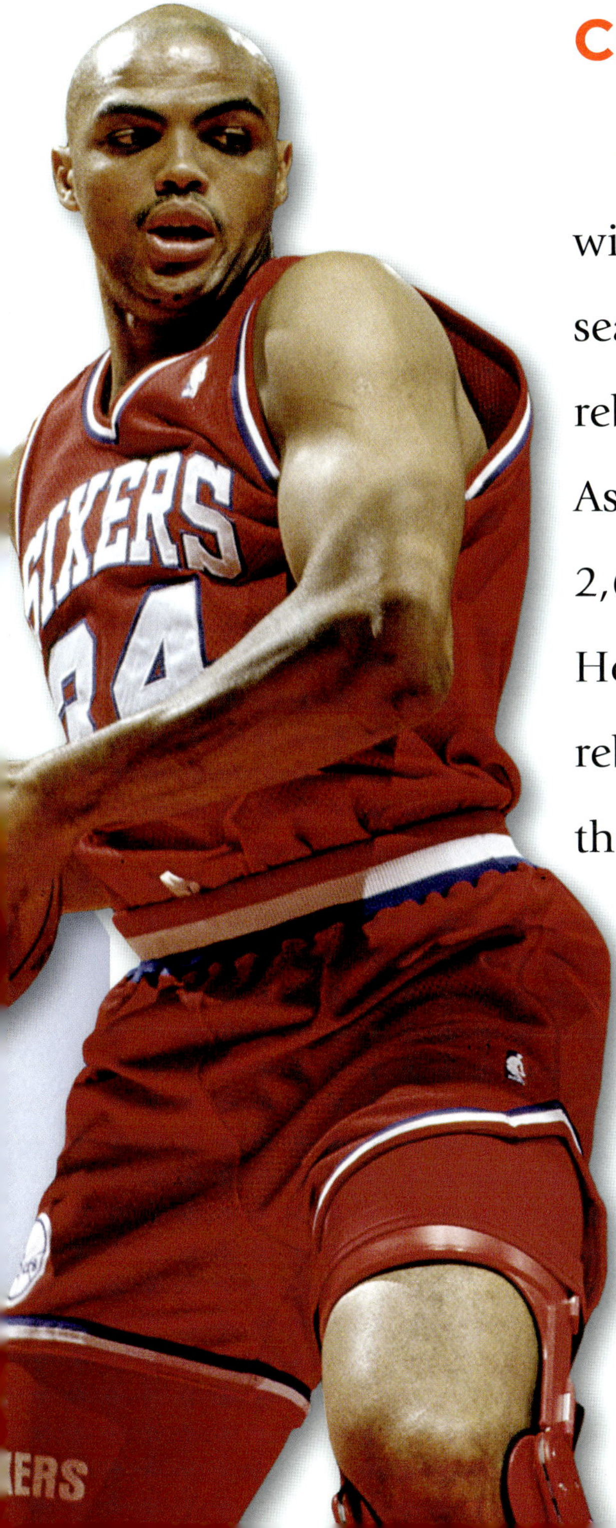

Charles Barkley

Charles Barkley played with the team for eight seasons. He was a rebounding machine. As a 76er, he made 2,688 **offensive** rebounds. He made 4,391 **defensive** rebounds. Both of those are team records.

Allen Iverson

Allen Iverson was a powerful scorer. He played 12 seasons with the 76ers. He had the NBA's highest scoring **average** four different years. He was elected to the Hall of Fame in 2016.

Players' Nicknames

Allen Iverson "The Answer"

Julius Irving
"Dr. J"

Joel Embiid
"The Process"

Sixers
21
Sixers
17

Joel Embiid

Joel Embiid is a rising superstar. In three seasons, he averaged 24.3 points per game. He also averaged 11.4 rebounds. He played in two All-Star games. Fans can't wait to see what he and the team do next.

76ers TIMELINE

1939
The team forms.

1955
Team wins its first NBA championship.

1963
Team moves to Philadelphia and becomes the 76ers.

1967
Team wins second championship.

1983

Team wins third championship.

2005

Iverson scores 60 points in one game.

2014

The team drafts Embiid.

2016

Team drafts Simmons.

GLOSSARY

assist (uh-SIST)—the action, such as a pass, of a player who helps a teammate to score

average (AHV-rij)—a number that is calculated by adding quantities together and then dividing the total by the number of quantities

career (kuh-REER)—a period of time spent in a job

defensive (de-FEN-siv)—relating to the attempt to keep someone from scoring in a game

logo (LO-go)—a symbol used to identify a company

net worth (NEHT WURTH)—the amount of money someone would have after selling everything and paying all their bills

offensive (OH-fen-sive)—relating to the attempt to score in a game

rebound (RE-bownd)—to take possession of the ball after it bounces off the backboard or rim

BOOKS

Flynn, Brendan. *Philadelphia 76ers All-Time Greats.* NBA All-Time Greats. Mankato, MN: Press Room Editions, 2020.

Gigliotti, Jim. *Philadelphia 76ers.* Insider's Guide to Pro Basketball. Mankato, MN: Child's World, 2019.

Whiting, Jim. *Philadelphia 76ers.* The NBA: A History of Hoops. Mankato, MN: Creative Education, 2018.

WEBSITES

Franklin's Story
www.nba.com/sixers/franklin_story

Philadelphia 76ers
www.britannica.com/topic/Philadelphia-76ers

Philadelphia 76ers
www.nba.com/sixers/

INDEX